RICHARD THE LIONHEART

A Life From Beginning to End

Table of Contents

Introduction

Richard I, commonly referred to as Richard the Lionheart, is best known today for his role in the legends and folktales surrounding Robin Hood, daring renegade and cunning thief of Sherwood Forest. In these stories, Richard is the beloved but absent ruler; his subjects all hope for the return of "Good King Richard" as they suffer under the tyrannical rule of Richard's younger brother, Prince John.

While the tales of Robin Hood make the name of King Richard familiar to many today, the spread of heroic legends about the twelfth-century king is nothing new. In the Middle Ages, a popular story related how Richard gained his name by defeating a lion and pulling out its heart. Even Shakespeare referred to this legend in his play *King John*, "Against whose fury and unmatched force. The aweless Lion could not wage the fight. Nor keep his princely heart from Richard's hand." Stories of Richard circulated not only in western Europe but also in the east, among Richard's enemies. Three Muslim historians of Richard's day recorded his conflicts with the great medieval Muslim leader, Saladin. These men portrayed King Richard as a fierce and formidable opponent.

Despite the image of Richard as a good king and a mighty warrior, the actual account of his life might surprise many readers. For instance, though renowned as king of England, Richard spent less than a year of his reign on English soil. In fact, Richard never even learned to speak English fluently. His real attention was focused on his holdings in France and on his crusade in Palestine. In these places, he was enmeshed in wars and politics, both as a king and knight charging recklessly onto the battlefield and as the central figure of complicated negotiations.

This book does not attempt to describe the complex politics of medieval France and England, nor to explain the history of the Third Crusade or explicate its horrors. Instead, what you will find here is a picture of King Richard himself—a story of the decisions, events, and people that influenced the course of his life. You will find the king who rebelled against his father and made a pact with his family's greatest enemy. Richard was a charismatic leader, but at the same time, he insulted and angered many nobles, making plenty of enemies. He had to flee through Europe in disguise, survived captivity, and never lost his love of battle.

Many historians have questioned whether Richard truly was a good ruler of his lands and his people. In these pages, you'll discover a king who was brave, a king who was daring and even reckless at time, a king who loved honor and glory. You'll see Richard the son, the brother, the sovereign, and the military leader. And as you read, you'll realize that no matter what questions historians might raise about King Richard, no one can question that the story of his life is an unforgettable one.

Chapter One

From Aquitaine to King of England

"Only the dead have seen the end of war."

—Attributed to Plato

The story of Richard I, the Lionheart, began in Oxford on September 8, 1157. His mother, Eleanor of Aquitaine, wife of King Henry II, gave birth to Richard in the countryside residence of Beaumont Palace. At the time of his birth, Richard was not marked to become the future king of England. He had two older brothers—William, who had died shortly before Richard was born, and Henry, who became the heir apparent to the throne. But despite not being born directly in line to become the next king of England, Richard's place in twelfth-century Europe was still significant. He was a Plantagenet, a part of one of the most powerful families of the Middle Ages.

Richard's father, King Henry II, rose to the English throne upon the demise of the heir of his predecessor, King Steven. Even before taking the throne, Henry's possessions and power were considerable. In the twelfth century, the area that is now France was divided into multiple provinces and feudal states. While most of these were nominally under the rule of the King of France, in reality, he controlled far less than a third of modern-day France. Richard's father, Henry, presided over numerous provinces; the most important of these were Normandy, Maine, and Anjou, all in the northwest of France. Henry consistently and successfully fought to increase the Plantagenet domain.

Henry's marriage to Eleanor of Aquitaine in May 1152 brought even more of France under the Plantagenets' sway. Eleanor was an intelligent, witty, and independent woman who stood to inherit power over the rich provinces of southern France, Aquitaine and Poitou. Henry was her second husband; in 1137, at the age of 15, she had married King Louis the Young of France. However, in the ensuing 15 years, this marriage had produced no son and heir for the French throne. Additionally, the relationship between sober, pious Louis and the vivacious Eleanor had been continually unpleasant to both, made worse by rumors of Eleanor's unfaithfulness to the marriage. Whether these rumors had any veracity is unknown, but in any case, both parties desired to bring an end to their unproductive and uncomfortable union. They succeeded in doing this in early 1152, citing consanguinity—a closer relationship by blood than the Church allowed in marriage—as grounds for the dissolution of the marriage.

What King Louis did not expect was Eleanor's almost immediate remarriage to Henry, a man 12 years younger than Eleanor. Henry was not yet the king of England at the time of his marriage in 1152, but with his and

Eleanor's holdings combined, the couple's control extended over almost two-thirds of modern-day France. Just a year later, Prince Eustace, heir apparent to England's King Stephen, died. Stories buzzed, contending whether he choked while eating eels, was poisoned, or was struck down due to divine retribution for some of his recent actions. For Henry, though, and for most of England, the cause of Eustace's death was less consequential than the result—Henry Plantagenet became heir to the throne of England. When King Stephen died in 1154, he left England in a state of disorganization and division. Henry, in response, sailed through a storm across the English Channel and was crowned king in Westminster Abbey on Christmas Day.

Henry's rule restabilized the kingdom, turning England into a valuable cornerstone of the Plantagenet domain. However, for the young Richard growing up during his father's reign, England was a far-off world. Though Richard was born in Oxford, he spent most of his youth in the south of France, mainly in Eleanor's court in the city of Poitiers. It was no secret that though Eleanor had given birth to two more sons after Richard, Geoffrey and John, as well as two daughters, Eleanor and Joan, Richard was Eleanor's favorite child and would be her choice to inherit her bountiful lands.

During Richard's childhood spent at his mother's court, the young prince's education began. His native tongue was the dialect of French spoken in Poitou, and beyond studying the basics of reading and writing, Richard also learned to turn language to eloquence in the manners common to the southern French court—in poetry, flattery, compliments, and song. Richard also absorbed the ideals of chivalry that knights were supposed to practice in the feudal society of his day. Poetry and songs painted knights as fearless, honorable, generous, loyal to their superiors, as well as defenders of justice and the Christian world. This idealistic image of a knight must have made a deep impression on the young Richard's mind.

Education was not assumed as an important characteristic of a knight. The Plantagenets, on the other hand, tended to emphasize the importance of academics and learning, differing from the culture of their time.

In addition to his academic education, Richard's progression toward knighthood and independence included serious training in military and fighting skills. In this area, he not only excelled in training but also seemed to find pleasure throughout his life. He learned to wield a sword, axe, and mace, and especially to master the complex skill of maneuvering a lance while on horseback. Horsemanship was fundamental to his development as a fighter, and Richard had to learn not only to fight both on foot and on horseback but also to defend himself. The military skills Richard learned involved knowledge of the tactics of war, development of military strategies, and the ability to direct and command his men in battle—all invaluable proficiencies as he moved forward toward knighthood and eventually, though he did not yet know it, toward the throne of England.

Richard's burgeoning skills would be put to the test before long. In 1172, when the prince was still just 14, he was enthroned as the duke of Aquitaine. While this formalized his place as the heir to Eleanor's lands, it also threw young Richard into the midst of the complicated and tangled political dealings of the time. This became most evident the following year, when Richard's older brother, Henry, left King Henry's court. Prince Henry, oldest of the Plantagenet sons and heir to the throne of England, fled to the court of his father's enemy, the French King Louis VII. Young Henry's action was a protest against the controlling nature of his father.

King Henry had already insisted on the unusual act of having a coronation for his oldest son to solidify the succession of the crown but had refused to pass on much real power to the crown prince. Henry, from King Louis' court, sent messages to his younger brothers Richard and Geoffrey attempting to convince them to partner with him in rebellion against the king. Whether because of Henry's persuasiveness, the princes' desire for greater power and wealth, their belief in their father's unfairness, or a combination of factors, both Richard and Geoffrey agreed to join Henry. Eleanor may have even played a role in egging her sons on; she did try to travel to join them but was caught and incarcerated by her husband.

Richard achieved full knighthood while in Louis' court, being knighted by the French king. After this, however, his successes were limited. King Henry's armies continuously defeated his sons', while Richard had difficulty mustering men willing to take on his father.

Divisions between the brothers and King Louis grew, and Richard gave up on the attempted rebellion just after he turned 17, a decision in which his brothers followed soon after.

Peace with King Henry did not mean complete peace, however. Richard gained more military experience fighting unruly nobles on behalf of his father in southern France, finally being rewarded by the king with the independent governance of Poitou. In 1183, Richard battled and defeated his brothers Henry and Geoffrey, who had conspired with nobles in Aquitaine against Richard. Despite Richard's initial victory, his brothers continued the fight with the assistance of King Louis of France. However, after several months of fighting, in June 1183, Crown Prince Henry became ill and died. With the death of Henry, the conspirators disbanded. His older brother gone, Richard was left as the oldest living son of King Henry II, next in line for the throne of England.

As heir apparent to the throne, Richard's conflicts within his family were not over. Around Christmas in 1183, King Henry demanded that Richard leave Aquitaine and instead take possession of two northern French provinces, Anjou and Normandy. Henry intended for Aquitaine to go to Richard's younger brother, John. Richard refused, and during the following year he fended off John's invading forces until King Henry stepped in to insist that the brothers make peace. The following year, the king ordered Richard to hand control of Poitou back to Eleanor. To this, Richard conceded, returning to his father's court in Normandy.

Despite this concession, the conflict between Richard and his father continued for years. In late fall of 1188, Richard surprised his father by swearing fealty to Henry's enemy, the young king of France, Philip Augustus. Negotiations between Henry, Richard, and Philip continued until late spring of 1189 when it became obvious that no conclusion was going to be reached. King Henry rode back toward his army stationed at Le Mans and was attacked en route by Philip. Richard's men joined Philip's in the attack on Le Mans, though Richard himself did not participate since his father was in the city.

After defeating Henry in Le Mans, Richard and Philip pressed their advantage, chasing Henry to different locations through France. Henry was not only under attack but was also becoming desperately ill. At last, he surrendered at Tours on July 4, 1189. He agreed to the terms proposed by his son and Philip on his deathbed. Two days after his surrender, on July 6, Henry died.

Chapter Two

Beginnings of a Crusade

"All things are ready, if our mind be so."

—William Shakespeare

In the midst of Richard's conflicts with his father, an event occurred that would shape his life and especially his reign over England. In November 1187, when Richard was staying near Tours, he received word from the Holy Land. Saladin, the fearsome founder of the powerful Ayyubid Dynasty and sultan of a vast realm centered around Egypt and Syria, had invaded Palestine in July. The slow-moving news had only made it to France months later. Richard, less than a day after hearing the message, made one of the most important decisions of his life. He took the vow of a crusader, promising to fight for the cause of delivering the Holy Land from the invaders. This pledge entailed serious responsibility: Richard would be held to his vow by the pope and was required to muster up an army to lead to the Middle East, a lengthy, expensive, and dangerous endeavor.

With the death of King Henry, Richard took up the scepter of England. Before he could begin work toward the fulfillment of his vow, he needed to make administrative preparations in his domains, as well as preparations for the army that would travel to Palestine. Richard's first step was to solidify his position as king. He sent word for his mother, who had been a prisoner under house arrest for 16 years, to be released. Eleanor began to travel through England, setting prisoners free and otherwise working to assure the nobles' and populaces' loyalty for Richard. Richard, meanwhile, met with Philip to settle their disagreements and begin preparations together for the crusade.

In August, Richard made his way toward England and London where his coronation would take place. The journey was marked by celebration all along the way. Richard rewarded many, including making rich provisions for his brother John in the form of the control over Gloucester, Derby, and Nottingham. He also saw to it that John married the daughter of the earl of Gloucester, even though the couple's close relationship as second cousins had earned the match the condemnation of the archbishop of Canterbury. Richard, determined to achieve what he wanted, pushed the marriage anyway. At last, in September, Richard arrived in London.

The coronation ceremony was held in Westminster Abbey on September 3, 1189. Despite the lavish display of power and wealth, the three days of celebration did not occur without tragedy. During the banquet following the ceremony, several of London's prominent Jews tried to gain access to the new king to present him with gifts. However, Richard's courtiers attacked them, throwing them out into the streets, where the delegation was even more brutally beset by the crowds. Riots ensued as incited crowds began to loot, burn, and kill in the Jewish section of London. The violence soon spread even beyond London into other provinces. Richard, as the king, had special responsibility for the treatment of the Jews, who were legally under royal protection. He worked to punish the leaders of the riots and attacks, but this retaliation came too late for many who lost their lives or possessions.

Following Richard's coronation celebration and the disastrous related events, the new king turned his attention to his crusade. His most urgent need was funds for his preparations. The sum required for ships, horses, provisions, and wages for his army was immense, and the amount Richard had inherited in the royal treasury did not come close to meeting this need. Richard, always a man of action, quickly devised another way of raising money. He relieved all government officials of their posts, selling those posts back to these men or others for a hefty fee. He also sold anything else that he could, such as improved charters for cities or royal security for monasteries. Men who had taken crusaders' vows could even pay to escape their commitment.

Richard's methods, while perhaps questionable on administrative and ethical levels, were quite effective in raising the money he needed. Unfortunately for England, in the process, Richard lost many of the capable officials whom his father had left in charge across the kingdom. In addition to this, the administrative system that Richard put in place for his absence divided rule of the country between two ambitious men—a recipe for serious problems.

After four months in England, Richard sailed back to mainland Europe on December 12. He had numerous steps to take there as he continued preparations. First, he met with France's King Philip. The two kings agreed on arrangements for the crusade, as well as setting their start date for April 1 of the following year, 1190. They also reached agreements regarding their land holdings, promising not to attack each other's possessions until the crusade was over. Richard, beyond this, made his brother John and illegitimate half-brother Geoffrey (not the same as his brother Geoffrey who had died several years earlier) swear to remain absent from England as long as the king was not present. This oath was meant to protect Richard's royal prerogative in his kingdom but ultimately would end up being modified at the request of Queen Dowager Eleanor, allowing John to return to England.

As preparations for the massive endeavor drug on, the kings were forced to push back their departure date until June, and then again until July. Richard used this time to consolidate his power in the south of France and build alliances there, slowly working to move his center of government from Normandy, in the north, to Aquitaine. As he traveled, the king founded two monasteries and routed a highway bandit who was accosting pilgrims on the Camino de Santiago. At last, as July began, everything was ready for departure. Richard met Philip at Vezelay, and the two kings headed out on their journey on July 4. The majority of the army would travel by ship, accompanied by five justiciars whom Richard had appointed to take command. The kings and their retinues, on the other hand, would travel overland. The journey itself would take almost a year.

Chapter Three

The Way to Palestine

"What has mood to do with it? You fight when the necessity arises—no matter the mood! Mood's a thing for cattle or making love or playing the baliset. It's not for fighting."

—Frank Herbert

Richard and Philip initially set off with the goal of reaching Lyon. However, their traveling partnership did not fare well for long. Upon reaching Lyon, the kings and their party had to cross the Rhone River, and disaster struck. The flimsy wooden bridge they were using to cross the river collapsed as some of their retinues, with heavy wagons full of supplies, marched over. A few people were killed, some were injured, and others were stuck, unable to cross until they located enough boats to create a temporary bridge. After this misfortune, Richard and Philip decided to journey separately. Philip would travel by sea, departing from Genoa. Richard continued the overland trek, heading toward Marseille. The two kings agreed to meet again in Sicily, at the city of Messina.

Richard's journey to Marseille was not in itself problematic, but he ran into unexpected difficulties once he arrived there on July 31. He had intended to meet his fleet there, but they had not yet appeared. Richard had no way of knowing that his men had been delayed, sidetracked by helping the king of Portugal fight against the Moors. King Richard waited, but soon a week had gone by with no sign of the fleet. He decided he could wait no longer. The king found ships to lease in Marseille and once again set out on his way. He traveled along the coast of Italy, stopping in Genoa, Portofino, Pisa, and Piombino. At last, in Rome, after making several complaints to the pope, Richard left his ships for horses and rode toward Naples. He arrived there on August 28, after almost two months of travel. From Naples, it was not far to Salerno, where Richard finally heard word of his missing fleet, which was on its way to Messina. The king, pleased with the news, continued his slow journey to rejoin his men.

Richard arrived in Messina at last on September 22. The following day, he made a grand and impressive entrance into the city, complete with blaring trumpets and clanging swords. Richard found Philip already waiting for him in the city. Soon after Richard's arrival, everyone was impressed by the show of affection between the two kings. The ruler of Sicily, King Tancred, also treated the kings with exceptional deference and courtesy. Richard's sister Joan had been the wife of William, the previous ruler of Sicily, and King Tancred offered to allow Joan to join Richard on the crusade. Richard, however, wanted a bit more—he asked Tancred to turn over Joan's dowry as well. Tancred refused. Though Richard let the matter rest for the time being, three kings and their armies could not lodge in the same city for long without the slow increase of tense undercurrents.

The tension broke into violence just a few days later, on October 3. Richard had commandeered a small monastery in which he stored his supplies, and the people of Messina were outraged. He had also left troops at the castle of Bagnara, just across the straight on the mainland of Italy, where his sister Joan was staying. Between these two actions, however, it looked possible to some that Richard intended to conquer Sicily. Fighting broke out in the city between Richard's men and the Sicilian citizens. Though at first the clashes were small, the violence quickly spread through Messina. Richard, not expecting the sudden turn of events, tried to put an end to the fighting by riding out and commanding his men to move back, away from the walls. His attempts were unsuccessful. He immediately changed tactics, meeting with King Philip and King Tancred to re-establish peace. This peace lasted less than a day before the fighting started once more.

Richard was enraged at the townsmen who dared to attack his army, and he quickly came up with a new and surprising plan. He would hold Messina itself for ransom until King Tancred met Richard's demands. Here Richard showed his tactical strength. His men, drawn up in position to attack the city, held their fire until the defenders' arrows were spent. They then returned a volley of arrows on the city walls, causing the defenders to dive for cover. Under the hail of arrows, Richard's men beat down the gates with a battering ram. Richard and his knights charged inside, speedily seizing key locations and taking hostages from prominent families; at the same time, others of Richard's men were busy setting fire to all of Tancred's ships. Using the hostages as bargaining chips, Richard maneuvered his way into control of the city, and from there worked out a deal with Tancred. The Sicilian king agreed to give Richard the additional money he wanted for Joan's dowry, Richard returned the city to the townspeople, and the two kings finally came to an agreement for peace.

Through the winter the armies camped in tents around the city while Richard and other noblemen stayed inside. Despite a brawl between different camps of sailors around Christmas, the established peace held. For Richard, the most significant event around this time was his decision to make a confession to the Church. In private, to important church leaders, Richard presented himself in a position of humility, barefoot and carrying thorns tied as scourges. What exactly he confessed is uncertain. Some historians have speculated that Richard could have been a homosexual—a serious offense in the eyes of the Church and medieval law—and at this time he may have renounced and asked to do penance for these sexual preferences. Whatever Richard revealed, he was declared absolved.

As the new year began, fresh news arrived in Richard's world. From England came word that John, whom Richard had allowed to return to the country, was causing trouble with the justiciars Richard had left in control. In Richard's more immediate proximity, his mother was attempting to come by land to meet him. With Eleanor came a young woman named Berengaria, the daughter of the king of Navarre, a province in the north of Spain. King Tancred, however, would not let Eleanor and Berengaria set sail from Naples to Messina. Tancred and Philip were aligned at this point, and Philip's sister Alice had long been betrothed to Richard as a part of political maneuvering. Philip suspected, correctly, that Richard had no intention of marrying Alice and planned to marry Berengaria instead. The three kings traveled to Taormina to negotiate. Along the way, Tancred, who still wanted Richard's support in other serious mattered involving his own claim to the Sicilian throne, produced letters to show that Philip was hatching plans against Richard. Whether the evidence was real or not, Richard was convinced. Tensions rose between the three kings, and Richard turned around and headed back to Messina.

At last, at the end of March, Count Philip of Flanders mediated a deal between the kings. Territory and money changed hands. Richard was released from his obligation to marry Alice. The Treaty of Messina also dictated that the French and English kings would share the spoils of the crusade, and it became the document that defined the relationship between their kingdoms during the remainder of Richard's reign.

On April 10, with conflict and negotiation behind them, the kings were ready for their armies and ships to depart. After stops in Crete and Rhodes, Richard's fleet approached Cyprus. The island had been taken by an unpopular ruler, Isaac Comnenus. When a few of

Richard's ships were wrecked in a storm, Isaac imprisoned the surviving men from the ships. Richard arrived on the island on May 6, and negotiations soon escalated into conflict. Richard was victorious and demanded Isaac's support for the crusade.

While in Cyprus, Richard also paused his journey for his wedding to Berengaria and her coronation, a lengthy celebration. Despite this event, Richard's dealing with Isaac was not quite over. The Cypriot ruler stole out of town shortly before signing his agreement with Richard. Richard took time to hunt him down, despite the arrival of urgent messages encouraging the English king to hurry to the Holy Land. After an unsuccessful battle from which Isaac escaped, Richard captured two of Isaac's key castles. He then made a discovery: in one of the castles, he had unknowingly trapped Isaac's daughter. Because of this, finally, at the end of May, the Cypriot ruler surrendered. Richard received abundant funding from the Cypriots and had gained a valuable harbor. At last, he was ready to sail on toward the Holy Land.

Chapter Four

Sea Battles and Sieges

"Nearly all men can stand adversity, but if you want to test a man's character, give him power."

—Abraham Lincoln

Richard and his fleet arrived in the Holy Land in early June 1191. He first attempted to dock in Tyre, but he found that Philip had left orders for the soldiers not to allow the English to come to land. Philip and his current ally, Conrad of Montferrat, did not want to take the chance that Richard would treat Tyre as he had Cyprus. Sailing onward the next day, Richard turned south.

Before long, his fleet encountered a strange vessel. Though the ship appeared French and flew the French flag, its occupants did not understand European naval communication, nor did they speak the French language. As a few men from Richard's fleet sailed toward the vessel, the ship drew up for battle and began to bombard the soldiers with its arrows and guns. Realizing the true situation, Richard ordered an attack. His galleys rammed the enemy ship, which soon began to sink. Those of its crew who were not killed were taken prisoner. From them, Richard gleaned valuable information.

The ship had been transporting soldiers to Acre, a city located on the coast at the extreme north of modern-day Israel. There, the crusaders had been fighting to take the well-defended city since August 1189, when Guy de Lusignan, the weak king of Jerusalem, made a poor tactical decision in beginning the siege. Philip's arrival in April with the French reinforcements and supplies had improved the situation of the attackers, but Guy had sent messages to Richard while the king was delayed on Cyprus asking him to come quickly. Now Richard finally made his way to Acre.

On June 8, Richard's fleet sailed into the harbor at Acre. The crusaders celebrated and cheered with fanfare and trumpets. The Muslim defenders in the city saw their hopes of survival growing slimmer and slimmer. Richard, with his bold and daring persona and talent as a military leader, quickly began to take control of the campaign. One method he used to gain power was to offer the men fighting for him a greater sum per month than Philip offered his soldiers, thereby gaining the allegiance of many of the crusaders at Acre. As a result, Richard had plenty of men to guard the most important of weapons, the siege machines. Philip's weapons, on the other hand, were repeatedly subjected to attack and suffered great damage due to the lack of guards.

Political turmoil and rivalry between the crusading forces continually influenced the European rulers' decisions. When both Richard and Philip fell ill, it was Philip who recovered first. He used this time to his advantage, trying to take back command over the invading force. Without Richard's agreement, Philip went ahead with a plan to assault Acre's walls directly. Unfortunately for Philip, this move resulted in disaster for his army, and the control of the field was left even more firmly in Richard's hands.

Richard, starting to recover, ordered the beginning of a highly effective catapult barrage of the city walls. He also oversaw the construction of military mines; tunnels dug under the walls. These tunnels would then be collapsed with the intent of bringing down a section of the wall. Between the catapult and mines, Richard's men made a significant breach in the wall. However, it wasn't enough for the army to break through into the city. The rubble of the walls provided excellent terrain for the defenders to fight against any direct onslaught. Richard, always clever and resourceful in war, made a new proclamation to his men. Anyone brave enough to sneak up and take a stone from the wall would receive a gold piece. This proved not to be enough of an inducement for such a high-risk, foolhardy task, so Richard upped the price. At last, his soldiers began to risk their necks to steal the wall itself. Not surprisingly, this plan resulted in extremely high casualties—more than the army could consistently sustain. Richard would need yet another plan if he intended to take the city. He began to plot for a final, decisive assault.

On July 4, Richard and Philip jointly refused a proposal of surrender from the battered city's defenders. The kings began their attack two days later, on July 6. Less than a week passed before the defenders again offered terms for their surrender. The first time, they had done so without the agreement of their commander, Saladin, who was stationed with his troops outside the city. This time, even Saladin agreed to let Acre's defenders barter for surrender. The English and French kings turned down this second offer as well, demanding more. At last, the defenders offered, in addition to relinquishing the city, to give the crusaders the relics from the True Cross previously captured by Saladin, pay a huge sum, release Christian prisoners, and leave behind their weapons and goods. Finally, the European leaders agreed to the terms. Before long, the banners of Richard and Philip were raised over the city as their soldiers celebrated. Duke Leopold of Austria, who had also taken part in the siege, attempted to raise his banner as well. Richard, incensed by this seeming attempt to encroach on his glory, did not stop his men from tearing down and vandalizing the banner—a serious insult to the duke, who would not soon forget it.

Despite this minor conflict, the evacuation of the defending forces occurred peacefully. Richard and Philip gave orders that the enemy soldiers should not be mistreated, and the men left the city in an organized fashion. The next issue confronting the leaders of the crusading force was the management of the conquered city. There were hostages who had to be guarded and property that had to be doled out between invading leaders. Churches were re-dedicated by Cardinal Alard of Verona. Nobles were rewarded for their services, though some were not content with what they received and returned home to Europe. Richard and Philip had to make decisions about the rights of businesses and merchants—decisions that would severely impact the economic future of Acre. Beyond these necessities, Richard was constantly involved in diplomatic negotiations with Saladin and other rulers.

As July neared its end, another notable change came to the leadership of the crusade. King Philip announced that he desired to return to Europe. There may have been any number of motivations for Philip's actions. He had already fought and would receive the benefits of being a crusader—benefits both to his kingly reputation and in the obligations the Church would now owe him. He would also be able to return before Richard, putting Philip at an advantage on European soil. Moreover, Philip had never had the same level of passion for military might and the strategy of warfare that Richard had. In any case, Richard met this declaration of Philip's intentions with relative indifference. Though King Richard would lose an ally on the battlefront, he would now be the only king on the crusade; with no competition for control, Richard could arrange every aspect of the war as he saw fit. After a variety of negotiations, settling remaining issues between the two kings and the effects of their conquests, Philip departed on the last day of July.

Richard now took complete command of the troops in the Holy Land. The results were soon unpleasantly bloody. Richard entered negotiations with Saladin since it was not Saladin who had made the official peace agreement at Acre. Saladin agreed to honor the terms of the agreement in full. This included payment of money and exchanges of prisoners and hostages from the two sides; Saladin requested that this should be done over a period of three different meetings.

At the first meeting, on August 11, a disagreement broke out. Richard's men claimed that Saladin should have delivered not just a certain number of prisoners, but specific prisoners. Saladin did not agree that this had been part of their terms. Richard, impatient, waited three more days as negotiations dragged on with no promise of a conclusion. Then he ordered action. The Muslim prisoners were brought outside Acre's city walls in chains—over 2,000 men. Richard next commanded his men to slaughter the prisoners. This decision, shocking to his contemporaries and utterly opposed to the ideas of honor in the practices of war made popular through song and poetry, goes entirely against the picture that Richard sometimes seems to have adapted for himself of the chivalrous knight. In addition, his decision meant that the number of his men who were prisoners of Saladin would die in exchange. But the exchange of prisoners had now been dealt with, and Richard was ready and eager to take his troops to new battles. On August 22, Richard led his forces south, leaving the city of Acre with its victories, conflicts, and tragedies behind.

Chapter Five

The Crusade Continues

"War is an episode, a crisis, a fever the purpose of which is to rid the body of fever. So the purpose of war is to end the war."

—William Faulkner

The march southwards was difficult for Richard's men. Two soldiers were reported to have been eaten by crocodiles, but numerous others succumbed to more mundane difficulties such as heat exhaustion. The soldiers marched along the coast, while the fleet moved alongside them, paralleling the journey on the sea. The trek continued into September, even as stores of supplies dwindled. Finally, Saladin decided to attempt to put a stop to the progress of Richard's army. As Richard's men crossed the plains near the city of Arsuf, it became apparent that an attack was imminent. Richard drew up his men into a strategic position for battle, but instead of attacking Saladin's forces pre-emptively, Richard waited for Saladin to attack.

On the morning of September 7, Richard's men were in place, waiting. Before mid-morning, the attack came. Infantrymen with bows and spears, Turks and Bedouin Arabs, rushed towards Richard's soldiers. In places, the attack broke through the front lines of Richard's foot soldiers, but could not push through the mounted knights behind them. Next, the enemy cavalry charged. They bore battle axes and swords—even more fearsome to the awaiting soldiers than the warriors who had come before. Their attack pressed primarily against the Knights Hospitaller, one of the premier fighting forces of the medieval European world. The Hospitallers wanted to break from their formation and return the attack, and three times asked Richard for permission to do so; the king continually told them to maintain their position. Richard rode through the ranks of the army, calling encouragement to his men as the defense held strong.

The king's strategy was to hold out until Saladin's forces had expended their energy in attacking, and then he would make a counter-attack. However, as the Hospitallers proved, it was hard for the knights to wait. Unexpectedly, two of the Hospitallers disobeyed Richard's command, bursting forward into the fray. Other knights saw them and assumed Richard had at last given the order to attack. This disorderly charge into the enemy ranks might have spelled disaster as King Richard's strategy fell by the wayside, but Richard, at his best in the chaos of the battlefield, rode straight into the fight to retake command. He pushed the charge toward a weak point in the enemy forces, forcing Saladin's men back in their surprise. As Saladin's soldiers regained their footing, Richard took a small, mobile band of knights with him and led an attack on another part of the field. The resulting confusion among Saladin's men decided the battle as his forces were driven to retreat. Richard's skill both as a strategist and as a commander, making decisions in the heat of battle, increased his renown. The victory at Arsuf was an impressive one and led many to hope that Jerusalem might be regained before long.

Soon after the battle, Richard moved his troops to Jaffa. Here they rested and also worked to build the city into a fortified stronghold. At the end of September, as Richard perhaps began to feel safe in his new base of operations, a sudden crisis occurred. The Feast of St. Michael was on September 29. Many took the chance to celebrate, including Richard. Along with a few other nobles, he rode out of the city to spend a day practicing hunting and falconry. As Richard stood beside his horse, working with one of his hawks, a contingent of enemy soldiers appeared and rushed toward the king and his men. Richard threw himself back onto his horse but was soon surrounded.

The story of the English king might have ended at that moment, but one of Richard's men called out in his limited Arabic that he was the true king, confusing the attackers. Several of the soldiers chased after this man, William de Preaux, giving Richard and his other nobles the chance to defend themselves. William was captured, and several others were killed, but the king and most of his men made it back to Jaffa. This alarming event did nothing, however, to change Richard's sometimes impulsive and reckless habits.

During the next few months, Richard continued negotiations with Saladin. Several of his most promising proposals centered around the idea of a marriage between Richard's sister Joan and a leader of the Muslim forces, Saif ad-Din—an interfaith marriage problematic in the eyes of many, especially the Church, not to mention Joan herself. As Richard struggled to work out an arrangement that would solve his problems of regaining the relics of the True Cross and the city of Jerusalem for Christendom, he did not know that other negotiations were taking place simultaneously. Conrad of Montferrat, the former ally of King Philip, was himself courting the favor of Sultan Saladin, proposing his own alliance with Saladin.

At last, after several days of meeting with advisors, Saladin chose Richard's offer over Conrad's. Richard, however, could not quickly bring about the marriage he had proposed. He had to ask Saladin for three months more, amid grumbling from many who did not approve of the terms of the suggested treaty. As the months went by, fighting continued on a small scale. Soon after Christmas, Richard moved his men. His troops were headed toward Jerusalem for the battle they had been anticipating. But as 1192 began, Richard evidently began to question his plan. He stopped, turning back to Jaffa to meet with his advisers once more. Despite the excitement of the troops as they finally marched towards their goal, Richard's advisers counseled that the king first take the city of Ascalon, to the south.

Severely disappointed, Richard's men received the news and changed the destination of the march. However, many French soldiers left the army and instead went to fight with Conrad. The army made it to Ascalon on

January 20, trekking through the worst of weather. The exhausted men found the city mostly destroyed, a mess of rubble and fallen stone. The task of rebuilding the city into a suitable outpost, adequate to support the upcoming attack on Jerusalem, took four long months. Richard also sought to use this time to settle disagreements between the crusading forces. He tried, unsuccessfully, to reach an agreement with Conrad. He also settled a fight between the Pisans and Genoese, whose conflict had escalated into battle back at Acre. Richard continued negotiations with Saladin, as well, having Saif ad-Din's son knighted.

Unfortunately for Richard, the news that arrived from England in April was not good. The situation there was becoming more and more serious, as Richard's brother John took more power into his own hands, nobles plotted against the throne, and money ran out. Additionally, King Philip, back in France, was preparing an attack on Richard's French holdings and was reportedly negotiating with John to make plans against Richard. Things looked dire, and the English king realized he might soon need to make an emergency return to Europe. Richard gathered the leaders of the crusade, asking them to choose a substitute commander to lead if Richard was forced to leave. Much to his chagrin, the vote went unanimously to Richard's rival Conrad. Richard, displeased, nonetheless went along with the choice of the council, and it began to look as if the forces might finally become more unified. But more bad news was soon to follow.

Less than two weeks later, two men surprised Conrad and attacked him with their daggers, assassinating the newly elected leader. The surviving attacker, captured, claimed to have been sent by Richard. While this assertion was likely not true, the assassination nonetheless succeeded in destabilizing the delicate sense of unity the crusaders had just achieved. Fortunately, a replacement was quickly found—Count Henry of Champagne married Conrad's widow and took Conrad's place as king of Jerusalem, with the consent of Richard.

Despite the complex political situation, the war against Saladin continued. Richard, waiting at Ascalon for the arrival of his allies the duke of Burgundy and the new king-elect Henry of Champagne, received news that Saladin was currently distracted with the suppression of a revolt. Never one to hesitate, Richard immediately headed out without his allies. His goal was a town just a bit to the south of Ascalon called Darum. On May 17, Richard began his assault on the city. The king even helped to carry the siege weapons from his ships to the camp. Darum, though heavily fortified, only withstood the heavy fire of the siege engines for five days before deciding to surrender. However, Richard did not accept their terms, and the attack continued. Military miners succeeded in collapsing a large tower in the wall. Richard's men were able to enter the city through the gap, soon completely taking over the fortress. With this victory, Richard had shown the world his power and military might, capturing the last of Saladin's important territories in Palestine. The English king now controlled the coast. All that remained was to recapture Jerusalem, the main aim of the crusade.

But apparently, by this point, Richard had questions about whether the retaking and holding of Jerusalem was a realistic goal. The king did not seem to be in a hurry to begin this next campaign. And soon, more bad news arrived from England. It seemed Richard's brother John had formed a deal with King Philip of France, and even Queen Dowager Eleanor was unable to stop her youngest son from continuing to create problems in England. Richard was left with a conundrum. He had made the conquest of Jerusalem his target, and to return to England now would be to capitulate on that aim. Also, if he left the Holy Land now, no final pact with Saladin would be in place. In June, Richard declared that he would not return to England immediately. He would take the greater risk and stay until at least Easter of the following year.

On June 7, Richard's army finally marched toward Jerusalem. Thirteen miles away from the city, he halted the troops. They waited there for a month, taking time to wait for further reinforcements and successfully sabotaging one of Saladin's supply trains. Though this attempt worked well, Richard and his counselors knew that there were no good water sources for the army in the middle of summer, and so to begin an all-out assault on the city now would be foolish. Even if they waited, there were pressing unsolved questions—the crusaders would need more men who could remain in the city after it was taken, and the long channel of supplies between Jaffa and Jerusalem would somehow have to be guarded. Richard, not having solutions to these problems, decided to focus on negotiations with Saladin rather than attacking Jerusalem.

In the midst of these negotiations, Saladin, certain that Richard's siege of Jerusalem would soon begin, had prepared his own attack. On July 28, he besieged Richard's captured stronghold of Jaffa. Before long, it looked like the defenders at Jaffa would have no choice but to surrender. However, as negotiations took place, Richard was on his way. Unfavorable winds slowed his ships' progress, but just before an agreement was reached, Richard and his fleet arrived. Once again, fighting began. This time, Richard's forces were victorious, and Saladin's men were driven back from the city. Richard plunged into the city with a relatively small group of knights and archers, regaining the stronghold for the crusaders. Saladin, his attempt at Jaffa thwarted, decided to try one last plan. Thousands of his men suddenly burst into the crusaders' camp. They charged towards Richard's camp, hoping to kidnap the English king. Unfortunately for them, an alert sentry had the chance to warn the king. Richard's men were organized, ready, and waiting, and came out of the fray decidedly victorious.

Both battle and negotiation seemed to be leading nowhere between Richard and Saladin. In August, though, Richard became very ill. He finally allowed someone else, the bishop of Salisbury, to attempt to secure a treaty with the Muslim sultan. The bishop succeeded in five days. The terms were not what Richard had hoped for: he would lose his base at Ascalon, which would be destroyed and not rebuilt for three years. However, he would keep other cities, and Christians would now be allowed access to Jerusalem. Richard, at last, agreed on September 2, 1192, and the treaty was finalized. Now Richard's main task in the Holy Land had been completed. As he began to recover, the king had a variety of other loose ends to tie up. But at the beginning of October, with parting threats to Saladin, Richard set sail to return to Europe.

Chapter Six

A Captive King

"In all things the Lord has turned cruel to me and attacked me with the harshness of his hand. Truly his wrath battles again me: my sons fight amongst themselves: if it is a fight where one is restrained in chains, the other adding sorrow to sorrow, undertakes to usurp the kingdom of the exile by cruel tyranny."

—Eleanor of Aquitaine

Richard's return to England did not go as planned. Rather than sailing straight to Marseille, the most direct route back, the king decided to land at Corfu, a Greek island. This may have been because he received a message telling him that if he landed at Marseille, his enemy, the count of Toulouse, would imprison him; however, there were alternative, relatively safe routes that Richard could have taken. Instead, at Corfu, the English king hired a band of pirates to carry himself and 20 followers along the Dalmatian coast, in modern Croatia. The pirates' sailing techniques through these dangerous waters were questionable to the point of being frightening, and Richard made a vow that if he survived the voyage, he would fund the construction of a new monastery or donate to an existing one. Upon landing, Richard and his men traveled disguised as pilgrims—a disguise made largely ineffective by their extravagant spending and by Richard's prodigious contribution toward the cathedral at Ragusa, where the men landed.

Therefore, Richard and his handful of companions once again took to the sea. This time, they did not safely make it to land, and their ships were wrecked somewhere in the Adriatic Sea. In early December, Richard and his men somehow made it to shore. Again, in an area where he had many potential enemies, Richard needed a disguise. This time, he called himself Hugh and posed as a merchant. The disguise was nearly as ineffective as his previous attempt. The men managed to travel a little over one hundred miles, to the town of Friesach, before being tracked down by a knight hired to capture Richard. This knight, Roger de Argentan, secretly loyal to Richard, warned the English king of the danger instead. Richard decided to attempt to steal away while one of his companions, Baldwin of Bethune, stayed behind and attracted attention.

King Richard left Friesach with only one knight and a serving boy as he rode for Vienna in haste. Behind him, in Friesach, the count of Goritz, hunting Richard, imprisoned Baldwin and Richard's other men. Within three days, the count discovered the truth about the situation. Richard was 145 miles away by that point, but he and his companion, William de l'Estang, were exhausted. Even though the king became aware of the renewed danger after his serving boy was caught, questioned, and released, Richard and William needed rest before they could go on. Two days later, Richard's serving boy was captured again, and this time he gave way under interrogation. Duke Leopold of Austria, whom Richard had soundly insulted at Acre, sent men to surround the house in which he was staying. On December 20, 1192, Richard had no choice but to surrender himself.

The English king became the prisoner of Duke Leopold, who soon entered negotiations about turning Richard over to the Holy Roman Emperor, Henry VI. Henry had reason to want Richard's downfall as much as Leopold—Richard was a rival who challenged Henry's domination of Europe and the Mediterranean, and many of Richard's allies were Henry's enemies. Beyond these considerations, the French King Philip was willing to pay royally to keep Richard from returning home, as he planned to attack Richard's holdings in France. Together, Leopold and Henry devised an extensive list of the concessions they hoped to wring from Richard.

A series of important meetings began. In England, Richard's justiciars met to try to decide what to do. They sent two abbots to attempt to find Richard and establish communication with him. The abbots succeeded with much difficulty.

Over the next two days, Richard and Henry met. Richard was given the list that Henry and Leopold had conspired to make. Some of these accusations, like Richard's part in the murder of Conrad, had likely been inflated by Richard's enemies. Richard not only defended himself but also refused to agree to the terrible conditions

Henry offered. Instead, Richard made an offer. England would pay an extravagant ransom for Richard—100,000 silver marks. However, Henry must stop King Philip from invading Richard's territories. If Henry failed at this, Richard would go free without paying the ransom.

Richard's problem, now, was raising the sum of money. He wrote to his mother and his justiciars with instructions. Not only should they seek money from the nobles (and keep track of the amounts each contributed), they should also take valuables from the churches. Richard promised to replace these holy items when he was freed. Unfortunately, when Richard had raised funds for the crusade four years earlier, he had already drained the kingdom's coffers; his administrators had struggled to simply make ends meet for the needs of the government while he was gone.

The justiciars needed another method of raising money, and they needed it quickly; their response was to design a new type of tax. Now, Richard's subjects were commanded to pay a quarter of their income each year in taxes. Even churchmen were subject to this tax. Money began to come in, and it looked as if Richard's ransom would be secured imminently. At Worms, in June, the terms of Richard's release were finalized and put in writing. This was bad news for King Philip and Richard's brother John, and they began working towards an agreement with Richard to protect themselves when he returned.

Slowly, the money for the ransom continued to be collected. Chests for the silver pieces were stored in St.

Paul's Cathedral, where Eleanor supervised the collection. However, the methods of taxation were disorganized—along the way, significant amounts of money likely slipped between the cracks, into various officials' pockets. Nonetheless, by mid-December, enough was collected that Emperor Henry proposed a release date for Richard of January 17, 1194. Though the event was later postponed to February 4, at last Richard was to be set free.

The formalities of the ceremony involved Richard giving up the English crown to the emperor, then Henry would return it to Richard—now Richard was nominally a subject of Henry's, and he would pay a sum annually in homage to the empire. The emperor also threatened Philip and John with retribution if they would not return the holdings they had taken from Richard. At last, after ceremonies and celebrations, Richard made his way back to England. His boat landed on March 13, and the king paraded into London amid much celebration three days later. Richard, his ordeal of captivity over, still had every intention of returning to the Holy Land to finish the crusade he had started. But unknown to Richard, this was not to be. His long absence had left his territories in disorder, and restoring his realm would be at the center of the remainder of Richard's reign.

Chapter Seven

The Last Five Years

"He was a man, take him for all in all. I shall not look upon his like again."

—William Shakespeare

Back in England, Richard had work to do. On Richard's entrance to London on March 16, he limited the celebrations to a single day. Prince John had tried to start a rebellion and captured several castles, but this did not take much time for Richard to make right. Most of John's followers were ready to desist as soon as they heard Richard was returning. But some remained, and Richard headed north, to Nottingham, to deal with them. There he found an army of dissidents waiting. The king put the castle under siege, building a gallows in sight of the wall and hanging those of the rebels whom he had captured earlier. When the rebels realized it was truly King Richard outside the walls, they surrendered. Before heading south again, the king visited Sherwood Forest, and he also traveled farther north to make a treaty with the Scottish King William. With these duties done, it was time for a real celebration. On April 17, in Winchester Cathedral, Richard was crowned king of England for the second time. This time, his coronation was symbolic—it showed the king reunited with his kingdom, and it made Richard's claim on the throne secure for any who had started to doubt.

Three weeks later, on April 24, Richard was on his way back to France. Eleanor convinced the king to forgive his brother, John. When that affair was concluded, Richard turned his attention to Philip. The French king continued to harass and attack towns in Richard's territories even now that Richard had returned. Much of the remaining five years of Richard's reign would be spent going back and forth in fighting and negotiations with Philip. Richard would never again return to England—the land that he ruled as sovereign, but which was not truly his home.

Money continued to be a problem during Richard's reign. Perhaps this is part of the reason why, in 1199, when a peasant discovered buried treasure on one of Richard's lands, it spurred Richard to respond with military might. The peasant's lord, Achrad, had claimed the treasure for himself. In turn, Achrad's lord, Viscount Aimar of Limoges, claimed the treasure as belonging to him. King Richard, as the viscount's lord, believed the treasure should, in fact, be turned over to Richard himself. When the viscount only sent him a part of the hoard, Richard marched to meet to viscount at the castle of Chalus and began a siege. Always part of the fray, Richard rode too close to the walls of the castle on March 26. A bolt from a crossbow jolted into the king's shoulder. Though the king escaped the battlefield, ordering his army to continue to assault, the wound was deep. A surgeon removed the bolt, but infection soon set in.

The wound grew steadily worse, eventually becoming gangrenous. Richard called Eleanor to his side and began to bequeath his possessions on his followers. To John, Richard left his kingdom. At last, on April 6 at seven o'clock in the evening, Richard died. He was 42 years old and had ruled England for 10 years. Five days later, Richard was buried at Fontevrault, where his father's body already lay, and his mother would be buried as well.

While Richard had died, the stories inspired by his life and reign would live on for centuries in songs, poetry, and tales. He would long be recalled in legend as the brave, noble, and daring warrior king of England—a figure only adequately described by his epithet, Richard the Lionheart.

Conclusion

Richard's ten-year reign over England has been viewed in different lights at different times. For historians and writers in the fourteenth century, relatively soon after Richard's death, the king was a hero. He was listed among the ranks of redoubtable leaders like Alexander the Great, King Arthur, and Emperor Charlemagne. On the other hand, since at least the 1800s, historians have tended to take a more negative view of King Richard. One scholar went so far as to call Richard England's worst king. Historians criticize Richard for his lack of attention to administrative and policy issues, as well as his excessive love of warfare and the excitement of battle.

Certainly, there were multiple sides to Richard. He was passionate about a cause that, right or wrong in today's eye, he believed in wholeheartedly. The Third Crusade dominated the story of his life. Because of the crusade, Richard's kingdom was left behind, over-taxed and neglected. For medieval Europeans, the crusades were the great cause of their time—they believed that a battle like the siege of Acre was as glorious and monumental as an epic story like the Trojan War. The rivalry between Richard and Saladin became the stuff of legend. Because of this, Richard had to be admired by the people of his day. He was, after all, brilliant as a leader and warrior on the battlefield, a picture of courage and valor. At the same time, this wide stage showed Richard's tendencies toward being arrogant, as well as sometimes bloodthirsty and hot-headed. So, perhaps the picture that we must finally construct of Richard is a multifaceted one, taking into account the attitudes of his culture and time. In the end, Richard was a king—a man who, through his decisions, good or bad, left an indelible mark on the world behind him.

Made in the USA
Middletown, DE
12 March 2020